MOZART

For Ezra

First published in Great Britain 1992 by
Victor Gollancz Ltd
14 Henrietta Street
London WC2E 8QJ

Design: David West Children's Book Design

A catalogue record for this book
is available from the British Library

The moral right of the author has been asserted

ISBN 0 575 05363 1

Printed in Belgium

Famous Children

MOZART

Ann Rachlin & Susan Hellard

GOLLANCZ CHILDREN'S PAPERBACKS
LONDON 1992

Nannerl was having a music lesson. Her father, Leopold, was teaching her. Little Wolfgang Mozart was watching and listening to every note she played. When her lesson was over he said,

"Please may I have a lesson, Papa?"

"You are too little, Wolfie!" said Father Mozart.

When Father Mozart and Nannerl left the room, little Wolfgang crept up to the clavier and played two notes. He smiled. The music sounded beautiful. Father Mozart heard him and came to see. Wolfgang was playing properly without anyone helping him. Father Mozart started to give his little boy music lessons.

Soon Wolfgang was playing as well as his big sister, Nannerl. He learned so quickly. His father was very pleased. But when Wolfgang started to write his own music, to compose, Father Mozart was delighted. No one could believe that a little boy of five could write such beautiful music.

Now Father Mozart decided to take his two clever children on a concert tour to Munich. It was a long journey. Inside the coach it was very bumpy. But still they had to work. Father Mozart made them practise on pretend keyboards.

As soon as they arrived in Munich, people began to talk about the clever little Mozart children. Dressed in their best clothes, they played for Prince Joseph. The concert was a huge success. Everyone clapped and gave them presents of jewels and lace. Father Mozart was very proud of them.

One large lady was so excited that she ran over to the little boy, picked him up in her arms and gave him a loud sloppy kiss!

"Yeuch!" said Wolfgang, as he wriggled away and wiped his face in disgust!

Back home in Salzburg, Wolfgang was so pleased to see his mother and his funny little dog, Bimperl. He had missed them very much. Wolfgang hugged Bimperl and then wrote a little minuet to celebrate his return. It was January 1762 - just days before his sixth birthday.

A few days later, Father Mozart gave Wolfgang a present. It was a little violin. That night when Papa's friends arrived carrying their instruments, Wolfgang ran

to fetch his own little fiddle. But Father shook his head.

"No, Wolfgang. You cannot possibly play with us until you have had some lessons and lots of practice." Wolfgang burst into tears.

One of Father Mozart's friends, Mr Schachtner, felt sorry for Wolfgang.

"Come on, Leopold," he said, "let the child stand near me. I don't mind."

"Oh, very well," said Father Mozart, "but remember to play softly, Wolfgang, so no one will hear you."

Wolfgang smiled through his tears and, standing next to Mr Schachtner, began to follow the music. Gradually Mr Schachtner played softly - still more softly - and then he stopped playing altogether. Little Wolfgang continued playing. Father Mozart could not believe his eyes or ears. How could his little boy play such difficult music without any lessons?

Their next journey was to Vienna and this time Mother came too. One day an important invitation arrived. It had a royal crest. Wolfgang and Nannerl were to play at the royal palace for the Emperor and Empress. There was such excitement! Clothes were washed and ironed. Shoes were polished till they shone like mirrors. Then they all climbed into the coach and set off for the palace.

The Emperor, the Empress and the royal children were waiting in the Throne Room. Wolfgang looked longingly at the children.

"Shall we be allowed to play some games with them?" he wondered.

First Wolfgang performed. Then Nannerl. Then they played duets together. The Royal Family sat motionless. They couldn't believe that all that wonderful music was being played by such a little boy and his sister.

While Mr and Mrs Mozart talked with the Emperor and Empress, Wolfgang and Nannerl played with the royal children.

"Whoops!" cried Wolfgang as he slipped and fell over on the polished floor. The little Archduchess Marie Antoinette helped him to his feet.

"You are very kind," said the little boy. "When I grow up I will marry you!"

After the children had gone home, their hands filled with gifts by the Empress, the Emperor stroked his chin.

"What a clever little boy! We must invite them again. I shall test him a little. I would like to find out if he is as good as he seems!"

Two days later the most wonderful clothes were delivered to the Mozart children. They were a present from the Empress. Wolfgang gasped. His suit was fit for a prince. There were white silk stockings, velvet trousers and a lilac jacket with a beautiful waistcoat. Nannerl's dress was rose with white embroidery. They wore these beautiful clothes when they went back to the palace the next week.

"Mr and Mrs Mozart, Master Wolfgang and Miss Nannerl!" announced the footman. As soon as Wolfgang saw the Empress, he ran across the floor, climbed on her lap, flung his arms around her neck and gave her a big kiss!

"What are you going to play, little one?" asked the Emperor smiling.

"I shall play my Allegro in B flat major," Wolfgang replied. He slid off the Empress's knee and ran over to the clavier.

"Very good," said the Emperor, "but first of all I wish to place this over the keys." He held up a large black cloth.

Mozart sighed. It made no difference to him. He could play the clavier without looking at the keys. The Emperor put the black cloth over the keyboard.

Wolfgang placed his hands on the cloth and played his Allegro perfectly.

"Well done!" cried the Emperor and Empress.

Father Leopold took Nannerl and Wolfgang to many different countries. One journey lasted three years and five months! Wherever they went, they gave concerts. Everyone admired them and gave them presents. They called Wolfgang, "Mozart the Wonder Boy"!

Wolfgang grew up to become one of the greatest composers of all time. Even today people all over the world love to perform and to listen to his wonderful music.

Wolfgang Amadeus Mozart wrote over 700 works including symphonies, concertos, sonatas and masses. He wrote 23 operas. The most famous of these are

The Marriage of Figaro

Cosi fan Tutte

Don Giovanni

The Magic Flute